7

GW01451594

salmonpoetry40

Publishing Irish & International Poetry Since 1981

Persecution

SOFIUL AZAM

Published in 2021 by
Salmon Poetry
Cliffs of Moher, County Clare, Ireland
Website: www.salmonpoetry.com
Email: info@salmonpoetry.com

ISBN 978-1-912561-99-5

Design and art direction: Patrick Chapman
Cover photograph by Jessie Lendennie
Printed in Ireland by Sprint Print

For those who were persecuted,
are being persecuted, and will be persecuted
in the name of race, culture, religion,
sexual orientation, politics, or anything else.

Acknowledgements

I am grateful to the editors of the following magazines where poems in this collection first appeared, some in earlier versions:

The Daily Star (Bangladesh), *Caught in the Net* (UK), *Cholla Needles* (USA), *The Quail Bell Magazine* (USA), *Better Than Starbucks* (USA), *Appalachia* (USA), *Harbinger Asylum* (USA), *Moledro Magazine* (USA), *Matador Review* (USA), *The Ibis Head Review* (USA), *The Literary Nest* (USA), *The Good Men Project* (USA), *Wilderness House Literary Review* (USA), *Pirene's Fountain* (USA), *The Ghazal Page* (USA), *The Cape Rock* (USA), *Oddball Magazine* (USA), *Drunk Monkeys* (USA), *North Dakota Quarterly* (USA), *Big Windows Review* (USA), *Artifact Nouveau* (USA), *The Stillwater Review* (USA), *The Elevation Review* (USA), *Postcolonial Text* (Canada), *fourW: New Writing 28* (Australia), *Le Zaporogue* (France), *Two Thirds North* (Sweden), among others.

Listing the writers and editors I am thankfully indebted to would be tedious for readers because I got love and help from almost every continent, mostly from North America. I should say Robert Pinsky (senior to me by forty one years!) boosted my self-confidence as a young poet. I gratefully thank my very good friend Daniel Thomas Moran, Allan Johnston who surprised me with his long review of my second book, and Sara who suffered enormously for staying with a poet under the same roof. Thanks to Patrick Chapman as my editor because he understood the very structure of this book; and finally but most significantly, I had some kind of desperation to feel at home under the roof of Salmon Poetry that Jessie Lendennie has been building for forty years.

Contents

PART THREE
EMBERS OF DISAPPEARANCE

PART ONE

Heat of Interrogations

On Being Asked What Life Is

Life's not a text on paparazzi's syllabus even though I know
I'd detest it if it were so. Life is still very simple. Say,
a tumbleweed keeps rolling on and on in the wind
until it finds soggy turf or a wet patch of earth
on which its propagules can germinate. Say,
a salmon keeps swimming on and on against the current
until it finds a safer bed on which it can spawn and die.

Life's not the Eat and Shit and Die triad. I find it
when I see an old man saving a youth of another faith
from outrageous hate crimes or slaughter during a riot.
Look at it, the tip of the wavering tongue
of a hungry young pregnant refugee waters. Its metaphysics
more far-reaching than light, and wherever you stay it's
everywhere God's alchemy. Sometimes shaky like agnostics

and the very next minute tending to belief only in logic.
Its mysteries grains of sand glazing in sunlight, stars
twinkling as when a couple makes love in a forest clearing
with fireflies stitching the perforated darkness.
Life is simple as uncertainty is certain at every turn,
be it beauty or dread engraved on our minds.
You know it oftentimes dares defy clever comparisons.

Coming of Age

I

I have no wisdom tooth yet. Does it mean
I don't have any wisdom? I know how it comes,
even fiercer than stampeding footfalls
of rhinoceros in the summertime savannah.
Cringing under its weight, I have all of my
adolescent years crushed like potato pulp
with its squeezed wetness drying out in the sun.

II

Before putting on a sleepmask, I think
about a few frayed lines of memory not very pleasing,
or about dreams stained by each individual's Cain.
Even as a child, I did atrocities like floating rat pups
in a coconut shell on a pond's calm water.
I hear their squeaks though I'm not degaussed
to such evils yet, drifting far from atonement.

III

I'm dorky, maybe a little insouciant.
What am I but an accumulation of memories,
each of which is surmounted with unsuccess?
Yet life is no scintillating snark. It never ends
with a supercilious air. I say it while I myself
am waiting to be rescued like a rat pup
kidded in a coconut shell to be floating away.

Today

Squeezing syllables for a drop of meaning is just a game today.
Should you think I'm more of a crazy slug limping for fame today?

If one sums up regrets over an amorous walking out in the rains,
people like snails will surely feel better off being lame today.

I'm tired of cooperating with dolts but I won't do it anymore;
for angels of non-cooperation – to say the truth – came today.

Many times I went on errands while dodgers sat back in pleasure
but I've decided to be the wildest horse none can tame today.

There's no time for freaking out. A male seahorse carrying
the female's eggs in his pouch and I are the same today.

Like Keats, I wrote sad poems like "La Belle Dame Sans Merci;"
I don't give a damn about who will be my merciful dame today.

Look at the last year's calendar where regrets towered over you
and you got flattened out in grief. Set them aflame today.

If you got fortune turned on time like a turbine in flood-tide
but naively pulled it off, there'll be only yourself to blame today.

Hit hard life's Gorgon-like temptress at every treacherous bend
and put – if you can – your remaining firmness in frame today.

Would you redline desires on this page white as an Arctic fox
and let go of what others may find in you to defame today?

I've too often blackened out my own dreams with extra ink;
it's time the day dawned with bright confetti of my claim today.

I've snatched a small victory over intimidation, it's party time:
like a caterpillar I will no longer lie curled in shame today.

Sofiul, say *Thanks for your sociable lies or sugarized concerns*
but don't be stupid to desire headlines with your name today.

The Capitoline Wolf

for Shayaan & Ariana

Today the sun — a white aubergine suspended without a stalk —
upended me with the surprise of its ordinariness.
Its light sneaked into my room through the curtain
and everything became bright as if I were seeing in years.
I realized that my sadness bottomed out,
and that I'd just as soon keep in check
memories of serving as a regent for this draconian feeling,
and find time to turn on end the head
of what had been mistakenly nurtured by myself.

Sadness always loves me for its sport killing;
yet I know I'll have my fortitude back like a river in the rains.
Even though I'm slow to happiness like a slug,
— no matter if rambunctious, quixotic or capricious at times —
I tell myself that I can afford to be happy
like a grizzly bear only having to feast on salmon
moving upstream through shallow creeks to lay eggs and die.
I need to act like a hiker does getting all he needs
on the wild shrubbery dense paths in Yellowstone.

I look at my expecting wife and kid still asleep.
They know common trappings and travails test my resolve
and I simply break apart in the blowing wind.
Capitoline wolf, should my kids be your teat-suckers, too?
Am I in a strange fit for soliloquies of an Elizabethan play?
Should I let what I have constitute my life
and wear my sadness like the inseparable skin on my flesh?
May the kids think gray leaves fall — if not defoliated —
so that green leaves have a chance to prove themselves.

Rain

I

At home while it's raining in the afternoon,
I kiss my kids and play, building a tent
with pillows and with an embroidered quilt.

Minutes ago, they did anxiously stick out
their hands through the balcony grille,
and felt the raindrops hit their tiny palms.

The cool electricity gave them goosebumps.
They also felt good about tulsi plants
in flowerpots responding to the wind.

Now they hear thunder rumbling too often
outside and snuggle up to me in fear. I love
every minute of it. I see lightning scrawl

a monsoon letter on the darkening sky
before I myself write one. My wife is cooking
rice-cakes best served with a paste of spices

and black cumin seeds, and getting ready
a bowl of puffed rice mixed with onions,
chili peppers, and mustard oil. Khichuri

on a rainy day-off is an added bliss.
My kids, tired with their joyful screaming,
will fall asleep. My wife and I will be talking

about our own childhood days at Granny's
till we doze off into each other's arms
with our eyes blinking at this idea

of such a blessèd togetherness, knowing
the rain will be pouring and thrashing
against windowpanes throughout the night.

II

I grew up picnicking in the Garo Hills.
In summer, I saw trees and clustered vines
dance in the wind and get covered with red dust.

One day we will go there, to see together
the rain falling and washing the dust
off their green foliage. I'll read out my poems

in there with the rain conducting its music.
If the rain stops before sunset, I'll take
my kids out to see how the valleys come alive

with frogs and crickets, and how leaves litter
the snaking mud-tracks through the hills
with a rainbow making a bridge overhead.

I'll tell them the names of wild plants.
We'll hear tailorbirds from their leafy nests,
also the endangered great Indian hornbills.

Each of our footfalls will skid dangerously,
and they will realize for the first time
how the wet earth smells. They'll be afraid

of how tiny leeches move, yet hanging around
all the more curious. I'll laugh away their fears,
assuring them of salt. Back in the cottage,

I'll plan an adventure for myself. My wife
will object to climbing the slippery hills
even with a sharpened bamboo. I'll give her

the creeps without taking any, even though
I know coming back to their arms feels
like a memory I'll cherish until I perish.

The Pond at Grandpa's House

On the pond with clusters of ivy gourd
   sparsely covering its reddish banks
and overhanging jujube trees
   lining them like tattered umbrellas,
I sail a raft of plantain trunks bound
by bamboo poles. A makeshift
paddle idle on my lap is brooding
   on the drift of things. Diving
from the raft like a carp leaping back
   into duckweed, water lettuce,
and watershield means braving
   a bone-biting cold even when the sun
is blazing down. Monitors lazily sunbathe,
   unmoved by the noise of hammers
and chisels for tapping toddy
   from date palms or by anglers
waiting with fishing rods. But I
   remain tensed like a hyacinth
worrying about the lowering water.
   Yes, such uneasiness stems from fears
that premonitions would come true.
   Soon the speed of grayness will crash
hard into all my time's greening up.
   Even if I get through to the last
stage, I'll be pipped and everything
   will fade to a gray I cannot
but accept. But still kites and fish eagles
   circle overhead, scanning each
square foot of hyacinths, their lush
   flowering thickets home to water rats
no drawback to the searching eye.
   Yes, I too know things continue
like minutes unable by a curse to stop.

The Scavenger

I often see him on my way home
   at night, fighting stray dogs for food
near the garbage

   spilled out at the street corner.
His life must be as serious
   as the night-hunt of a fruitarian

scavenging in roadside garbage.
   He must have trained himself
through the toughest

   of austerity measures. And perhaps,
with the rains setting in
   on the slippery tail of a busy summer

coming up as sudden as an accident,
   even the thought of a bug-infested bed
is for him a luxury. As his fortune

   wriggled out of his fingers long before
like an eel, every good thing seems
   to be a pain in the ass,

and the smell of fried
   coriander seeds a whirlwind
of chili powder in the nostrils.

   As for his tummy, it doesn't swell
with food; it rather gets
   bloated with ulcerous gas.

Listen, what comes out of it
doesn't smell at all like eau de cologne
killing odor-causing bacteria.

His body doesn't make
any difference, either. Who knows
why his fate turned and taught him

how to accept humiliations warmly
and make himself at home with them?
For it's all written on the wrinkles

of his forehead. Perhaps he's confronted
them many times, telling
"I don't need you. I have enough

memories of you to live with."
But they stay on
like iron filings in a magnetic field.

Every humiliation
– as far as I can imagine –
is scarier than when you get trolled

on the web or when you lose
a libel claim in court. At times,
he's broodingly quiet

as when a convict knows there will be
no reprieve. Yes, you can take
an educated guess

on his life or how it all started off
like a seed from dogshit
germinated on a pavement crack.

In the Discomfort Zone

Come out of your comfort zone
  and explore the world
but I have never been there.
  In the discomfort zone,
a larva loses hope before its time
  for pupation; no desire to be
on the wing to see the world from above.
  Snippets from its unfinished biography
seem to be either lies or half-truths
  like the alphabet falling on hard times.
Discomfort is a left-over meal for me.
  I who never vilify anyone but myself,
I who only shop around
  for vagaries of my mind
that remains as ostensibly unruffled today
  as when it was first sensed
in some bruised part of my body,
  have been living in the discomfort zone
where everything's been around for years
  but beautiful like the last days
of a terminally ill patient. I know
  beeping out the F-words
won't get me to the comfort zone.
  Had I lived in there, I would have
discarded it to explore the world
  as a fisherman scans the winter sea
before diving into it to catch eels –
  like getting back to the discomforting
world of which I have been a part
  all these years, so natural no one
doubts my owning a tiny inferno in it.

On the Verge of Bipolar Disorder

Is it a luxury when refugees with babies
  swaddled in their shawls are
running from the incoming bullets
  or waiting for who knows what
chemical attacks to be exterminated
  while the "morally unfit" have
never been crushed under wheels?
  Is it time to eat into the personal
so that life is no more a non-
  disclosure agreement? I, who am
gentle with strangers but fiercely
  emotional with those I love,
ask all who really care. I'm having
  a multiplicity of feelings coming
from the areas I never knew existed.
  The biggest question fronting up
is how to make sense of this very life
  riddled with non-answers
when the right hand doesn't know
  what the left is up to or how it fails
to remember all the left's kindness
  to it. No union of words to form
a sentence or no punctuations
  to pause for a thought: this new
normal is outflying the stormy wind
  of summer. The priority is to survive;
to thrive – just an extravagance when
  I'm rumored to love being pillowed
on poetry's heaving chest of sadness.
  Even sadness is suspicious of me;
so it gets all its watchdogs to audit
  the last remnants of my trust in
happiness – a breakthrough by accident.

In Yellowstone

I'd have backpacked there had I been that young.
I see its beauty from across the continents.
Also, I watch a thieving coyote
take an otter's catch of a cutthroat trout

fished through a little opening into the ice.
After the long hibernation a grizzly
or a black bear seizes the wolfpack's
kill of an elk in spring or early summer.

A bald eagle swoops down on a red fox's
meal of a vole or a shrew caught
after its repeated foxy jumps into the snow.
A mother osprey from its high perch looks on.

The bison herd grazes nonchalantly for the moment
if not getting warm near hot springs, geysers
or bubbling mudpots in mid-November.
Common loons swallow eggs of trout

from the lake's tributaries; trumpeter swans
also dip their necks underwater. Boreal
toads and spotted frogs struggle in bullsnakes' jaws;
prairie rattlesnakes and garter snakes

do not simply flick out their forked tongues.
Bighorns fight for their right to smelly rumps
on the rugged mountain slopes;
both bull moose with their palmate antlers

and pronghorns fight during the rut.
After resting too long in their dens,
bobcats, lynxes and cougars yawn out,
about to roar for yet another fresh kill in days.

A Jar of Sand and Little Pebbles

On my table an airtight jar with silver lid
stands upright. It's filled with little
pebbles with muddy sand immersed in water.

The water like everything else is
from a shallow stream in the Garo Hills
north of my hometown. I spend hours

looking at it and wonder why it feels
very dear to me. It never talks back to me
when I talk to it as if to the boy I was,

long since lost while growing up. I keep
looking at the jar, not as precious as
something dug up from an archeological site.

Does it invoke the memories of trekking?
Or is it because I'm very slow, not
getting any younger while my mind's still

a greenhorn's green? I feel the increasing
vulnerability of my bones if I think of
the perpendicular height. Then I sink

into the bottomless deep of discomfort.
My flagging spirit tells I have lost
lots of unlosable things – like sand

slipping from under my feet at a low tide.
Now I'm a juggernaut stuck in a deep rut.
But something deep inside whispers:

there might still be a way out somewhere.
I keep looking at the jar as if a Pollock
at one of his paintings still slowly drying.

Nearing Middle Age

I

Before you plan a workout to get back in shape,
you'll find it's been half a life now. Even the pains and pleasures
  of parenting do not count when you are left with underachievement
and the feeling of getting rationally insane about it.
  It's the rust that slowly eats your iron-like firmness. A spliff
or booze can't drive it away. While waiting to be happily done
  with all of that, you can't expect even an apology from yourself
for not moving past differences to get along with those
  whose Midas touch — as you love to spread it in your circle —
turned all your precious feelings into the alchemists' sought-after gold.
  Your freedom will be that of a horse as free as it can be
in a paddock, and you can regain a bit of your soberness
  by talking to irresponsive fireflies after dusk. Even then, you will
feel the rust growing bigger and bigger with the salt from your eyes.

II

In the dark, ask yourself what it takes
to rein in your mood swings and stop
  your eye-rolls at your own mansplaining.

Don't gape at all these like a gavial
with its jaws wide open for a victim.
  In the end, you'll learn the victim is yourself,

and your retaliation will create no consequence
while for some time you can enjoy
  at your own peril the perversion

of a dirty old man watching young girls' nipples
protruding against slinky T-shirts; for that,
  no one needs to be a boob critic.

But it will follow that you are no longer young,
just a rugged boulder about to crash down
  at the foothill. Don't even expect

the luxury of being weirded out to get
a confirmation letter of youth in the mail.
  In the gathering dark, you can strike up

a conversation with ghosts of hatred.
But don't be mortified at yourself
  for what you are, like a bunch of jerks.

III

How to take the signs that you are nearing
middle age is harder than ducking

a firestorm with who you lived so long
  and made babies once beautifully helpless,

  now sadly better off unaided. Things
won't let you forget that you are aging,

maybe arthritis or those youthful midnight
  acrobatics on the white page or you being

  no longer unfazed by any perpendicular
height. Because it's a time when fears

of the end spread like metastasis, this lifelong
  matchup of virtues with vices won't give

  you peace, nor will your repentance
for being a brute playfully killing skinks

and sewer rats with brick bats. Yet you have
  the propensity to feel as if you lost

  all your innocence at gunpoint, but no
reimbursement! Because you have so

many roads still untaken and your legs
  not the most enduring, you will feel

as if you were a warthog, being chased,
not so sure about charging with its

curved tusks at the lion; what would you call this,
defense strategy or final bravery?

Earth and Windows

Born in cold January on the mud-floor of my Granny's
storehouse bamboo-walled and roofed with corrugated tin,
  I thought I was getting unmoored from attachments
  as if I were looking out a window of a high-rise
only to see a piece of driftwood float down the river.
But I was wrong from the start for I couldn't see
  myself tied up with the invisible ropes of belonging.
  Whatever Athenians thought, an owl's innards
cannot tell of one's destiny for sure; this is superstition.
I would rather continue peeling it like an onion and cry.

Whatever the specifications of the situations I am in,
I think of this uncertainty as custom-made, only deeply
  whenever I'm stuck in a traffic jam on Green Road
  where goings-on get all the more difficult in the rains.
If this is so, there's no use hollering about a ticket
to heaven. The pain I am in today is getting me
  hungrier for the endurance I might need for tomorrow.
  This hard-won consolation tastes bitter for I've always
been on the receiving end, and it can only trigger
my instability, anyone's ghosting no less for the worst.

The hurts I'm given as gifts by chauvinists are cumulative
even though I implored their mercy. I don't ever relish
  the singular idea of being rooted in just one spot;
  I rather feel like a rhizome branching out new roots
from its nodes, trying out its various potential climates
for the plurality is itself a self-renewing adventure.
  Losing faith in those too preachy about the singular,
  I prefer to be an unpaired jerk lusting for the plural.
If I say this planet is where I began and my windows
open into the universe, would I be allowed to belong?

PART TWO

FLAMES OF DESIRE

Make Love, Not War

The lack of what we lack is a lack
  stitching our desires together,
in between our twisted bodies
  rippling with a tide of togetherness,
anticipating its falling back in fear.
  The world is what it likes to be
but we do not want it to mirror
  the conflicts that multiply around us.
Life is never without them.
  Yet we buried our doubts
we promised each other we would
  never let any of the smartest foxes dig up.
But we find to our horror:
  doubts are unstoppable like slithering
serpents into Behula's chamber.
  This anxiety like a hand scraper
smooths out the iron of our trust.
  Stories of betrayal read well
but they don't fit into your life
  like a mortise and tenon joint.
As I open my arms for a hug,
  come to me like iron filings.
Waste no single minute before we make
  love like this world ends right now;
and at least pretend in good faith
  that the sad faces of refugees
fleeing the devastations of war
  will find love like a revelation.

Sides of a Coin

I. *The Amorous Letting*

Look, this pair of five-tined sparkling harrows
is itching to plow outright, with a volunteer's charity,
never to rust out in a devil's idleness.
Let it lovingly till every inch of you.

Let this unhurried slug climb and circle
your heaving peaks and check what it's standing on
and explore all it can on its own,
to end with sipping from your volcanic crater.

This shark dives best into the briny deep;
so you'd better let it swim until it gets dizzy and rests.
If you put its expecting muscles under too much stress,
it might sadly float belly-up in the end.

II. *Memory*

In my memory the city in which I made love to you
still remains silky-smooth and perfumed.
When you muscled me through your inner lips
little by little with the flexibility of a snake's jaws,

I had a feeling: the prey's dissolving
with the digestive juices you had in your love.
In reality I'm sadly undigested, and everything's arid –
a fresh kill left by mistake to rot and dry in the desert sun.

What Could Have Happened
on a Spring Afternoon?

I should have kissed you on a spring afternoon
when there was a gust of wind ruffling your unbound hair.
Your eyes didn't have the stony stare, and the sunlight fell on you
– streaking through smudged, south-facing windowpanes –
to add up to the beauty of your unpainted face.
I was looking at you and anxiously thinking of you.
Were you thinking of what I was thinking about?
You teasingly squeezed orange peels into my eyes.
I suspect your chest was heaving too much like waves
with the anticipation of what would follow next. Many things

could have happened: I could have you roped off by love –
the most tightening, though a little frightening,
of all ropes in the world. I could have held you
the way the destitute do their bundles of last things before guns.
I could have entered you the way ancient men entered caves
to save themselves from the outside world's insecurity
for I never wanted an eavesdropper's booze or bolster
on a lonely bed. I didn't have a good-for-nothing's supinity
or a namedropper's vanity. Yet only I could have
made you a river by jumping into you. But I shrugged off

each of the options carefully like an intelligent fool,
thinking I was stepping dangerously beyond borders,
awaiting snipers' bullets out of nowhere. I remember your eyes
about to come alive with the tide of your tears
and your lips quivering to word a timid sentence with love.
Maybe time was against us, and finally it has wedged
a gulf widening ever more in between us and set us
two separate islands far apart on our different courses.
And now there's nothing else for me to get past being terrified
except one thing at last – a poem punctuated by regrets.

Abortion

In a quiet tree-sheltered corner by the park's walkway,
we sat grim-faced, no one looking at us, yet none
of us daring to break the silence. Tears on our eyes
were on the verge to fall but not falling, as if
they were waiting to ask for permission to fall.
Joggers jogging, kids hollering, and birds twittering
on the trees' slender twigs hanging over the lake:
everything seemed to be in order, spanking new
as housecleaned, yet it seemed a phial of liquid silence
was poured on such a nice morning like this.
We scarcely looked at each other, and talking

seemed to be under a hypnologist's trance:
no paronomasia nor a polyglot's charisma for sure.
I knew she had to kill it – the embryo of our secret love,
and I didn't have even pleaded with her to keep it.
This treacherous embryo almost conspired
to unveil everything we did behind the smoke screen;
we had to get rid of this brutal silence-breaker.
The abortionist did a good job indeed. But bloody
we were, killers of a dream or a dread spring-cleaned
and aired out to the light as its return to normalcy.
How many times I screamed to myself! But the wind

– a preserver of so-called sanity on the surface –
took them away, uninstructed. Then to her kids
and her hubby she went, leaving me on the park's bridge,
alone in the crowd, a perfect setting for another Munch.
I stood there in the morning sun and tried to glean
myself from my likeness on the lake's emeralds
but ripples made it harder for me, as if meaning to say:
You bastard, I won't even pose to be a mirror for you!
I thought what a father I could have made! I wished
ripples had creeped up on this so-called straightness thing,
only to break through its siege over the centuries.

Krishna's Return Home

I

As I reluctantly walk out of your woolen warmth
far worthier than the promise of a kingship
in heaven, I see washing on the line under the sky
with a few stars peeping like pot-bellied spies
through the curtains of dark clouds. These stars
are tempting coins set as traps on my path.
All of a sudden on your backyard I feel
something against my face like a cold spidery web.
I look up and see it's your wet sari, flapping
and brushing my anxious face. I feel this is
your assuring kiss for a goodbye. Before he comes,
I must wade through marshy mud leeches
to come home to my hut of paddy sheaves plaited
against thrashing rain, cold and uncared-for.

II

With a few drops of blood as charity for leeches,
I reach the deep-dark copse behind your house
where we made love so many times under the moon –
our only faithful witness. I bring out my flute
but I don't feel like playing a tune for the moment.
Then rain starts and it gets heavier as minutes go;
it seems no letdown of the rain for a foreseeable time –
and me wavering as if a mortal undecided
between heaven and hell. This rain is a hellish hoard
of hails and thunder sewn by the zigzags of lightning.
I'm waiting, a rain-soaked crow. And then the rain
stops. As I start off, I stumble on a puddle of rain
water, getting my forehead bruised on thorny weeds.
I'm returning home with your fresh memory and a bruise.

Seven Rough Sketches on Smoothness

I

I'm afraid something shrinks
like a homeless street urchin –
close to hypothermia.
He needs, above anything else,
the care of your warmer, deeper lips.
Take him up from there,
let him feel snug
in the January cold.
Pull him in and feel his pulse beat.
Give him a bit of your inner warmth
and your mineral-rich water
to quench his age-long thirst.
He feels dizzy, though,
prone to retching in the end.
He gives you an indulgence in orgies,
a pleasure in charity at least.

II

Unforgiving, brute
as the April sun,
you rain drying-up rays on him.
You melt his dreams' wax,
meant to be light in the dark.
Come up like a storm
with the disheveled hair
of rain clouds over his arid horizon.
Let him till your arable patch
and you'll see it
cropping up with golden harvests.
Some could be stored for nostalgia.
Like I said, it will make do
even with a shirker's
clever excuse you cook up
for your resistance check.

III

A standing ovation at a coronation —
an outright disturbance
for his blood's ardent rush
better felt in a warm retreat.
Don't bother to be a liberal
oblivious of where he'd end up.
Rather be a control freak.
Make him a dog on the leash.
Remember a house is not
a home without a licking dog.
He's only afraid
of your resistance military build-up
along the border
of your other possibility
worth a thousand showers
on deserts' arid dunes.

IV

Use him as your constant ploy.
You can expand dominion
as far north as the Terrestrial North
of his heart's desire.
But be kind enough
to cloak him in your flesh —
far more viable than a fur coat.
Only then can he hope to defy cold
even in Siberia. He doesn't mind
being of use to you until death
as a guinea pig
for any of your lab experiments.
He doesn't wish to free himself from you,
he wishes to free himself
only through you
like water through sluice gates.

V

He's a little short on cash,
not on dreams of himself
always ending up in you.
No matter how weird it sounds.
He has seen how city trucks
unload at garbage drop-off sites.
Since then, he's dreaming of himself
dumped in you for good.
Even his future grave lies *in* you.
What's heaven? He doesn't give
a damn about whatever
gods and prophets tell. Yes,
heaven *is* the time when he fuels
every inch of you with thrills,
his mouth clutching at nipples
as a drowning man's straws.

VI

Once on a sudden visit
to his ancestral village
during the monsoon rains,
he saw farmers wade through mud
– weeded-out and buttery –
to sow green seedlings in rows.
Right at the moment,
he thought of planting himself
as a seedling deep inside of you.
I think he might have assumed
he would have
all the nutrients from you.
He'd be the father and the son –
a 21st-century chronicler of incest.
He had always been "a scorner of the fields"
as Lamb described by Wordsworth!

VII

He doesn't like mountains
nor Arctic icebergs.
He starts shivering with cold
even at their slightest mentions
except when you're mentioned.
Your name is warmth itself.
But by and large he prefers
high grasslands, roundish
and topped off with your nipples
instead of peaks. In fact,
his tongue even waters
at the mention of your breasts —
taut beehives in the Sundarbans.
But who's he aspiring after Sanskrit poetry?
An unlikely entry in the *Who's Who*
of lusty connoisseurs?

On a Date Night

I did never fall in love with you, rather always wanted
to rise in love with your moon against the dark,
for love's never been a swatch of no ground for me.
Look at this living portrait of a poet with wavy hair
and the cleft chin, who has waited too long a time
for this very date night. This man your man
with who you made the world taut with dreams

waits for your smile not innocent nor the sexiest,
somewhere in between, and the mystery about it
unfolds like a promise wrapped in despair.
Your teeth a pair of silver razorbelly minnows
and your lips banks of a canal before the drought.
Then what passes through me without your knowing
is a storm at full blow, like the epiphany I wait for.

When we fight, it seems we are equally imperfect
but please let no one say the split is imminent:
our imperfections are our trophies of endurance.
You are not a Bengal loach nor my childhood's
banded gourami I used to keep in a glass jar,
especially when rain flooded our backyard pond.
Be the poem I'll end up writing every time in loneliness.

How Can You Resist Me in My Dreams?

I have never wanted you to know I love you the way
rain doesn't want trees to know it loves them.
I want my love to remain as a non-consensual act
for I want nothing in return. I only dream of you.
How can anyone resist me in my daydreams?
But if you torture me in these teasing fantasies,
I'll sure blow into your blouse in your nightmare

the orange hairs off Bengal velvet beans' seed pods
I myself went to bring from the Garo Hills or rub
the stinging nettle leaves from our backyard bush.
Then you'll know how much wickedness still remains
of the child I was 30-odd years ago. But in case
you love me, I'll massage away the tension,
pressing African dream herb seeds on your muscles,

and you'll fall asleep, of course in my imagined arms.
I visited the hills many times for these seeds
though I never let them drift for dispersal by water.
Oh no, all this bullshitting doesn't make sense
for I won't let you know I loved you for a moment.
I don't know why I flee like a grassbird scattering
in flight when a Bengal monitor nears its nest of eggs.

Who Doesn't Want to Make Love to Someone's Wife?

I

Right from the word *Go*, I knew well that I'd have to
   cut down on fantasies, that I might even have
to hide from society's moral pretension
   the process of pupation to get transformed

as a well-loved butterfly. You know people do wrongs
   lovingly or so they say. Yet while it's
not totally wrong, I'll go the extra mile for it;
   who doesn't want to make love to someone's wife?

What it boils down to is that its manifold answer
   might sound harsh. Could I borrow you?
I promise you will be returned unhurt to him
   who'll know nothing of rain's work on a taro leaf.

It's not a long-distance love affair, rather a thrill
   of honey collection from a wild forest. Rekindle
your fantasies about how or when love is enjoyed at its best.
   Let's do it in whatever ways we can.

II

I'm sure both of us have never been to a vineyard.
  Yet the moment someone utters "vineyard"
I start dreaming of making love
  to you who I'll do everything to live with forever,

on a vineyard's drained soil
  littered with gray leaves and pruned canes,
yes, of course, between rows of vines full of red grapes
  with the sunlight making them look like rubies.

I also want to do it with you under the moonlight,
  between rows of vines with clusters of ripe grapes
staying covered except for the star-spangled sky,
  before harvesting grapes rich in color starts in late summer.

But I don't think the owner of any winery
  will let it happen. Maybe you to whom I hope this won't
seem to be a one-night stand know
  most of our fantasies might remain fantasies.

Could I Borrow You, Please?

With a killer smile, you flaunt your lovely curves
in a form-fitting dress, and now every other thing
takes a backseat. Now I must not be shy anymore
for the sky becomes the limit for my shamelessness.
Wriggle into my arms and twine around me
like a snake; and I'll declare my whole world is yours,
yours alone. I promise your life will no longer feel

like a parched tongue touching the walls of the mouth
for a little moisture. Your calm skin will throb
like the surface of turbulent waters in the storm.
Your frigid backbone will enjoy the sweetest thrill
of a seismic quake very high on the Richter scale.
My ex-girlfriends said I had always been a genius,
a great improviser, when it comes to the art of kissing;

I promise I'll sure teach you the tongue dance.
My lips will come down your throat to your breasts
like a train slowly but all the more gracefully;
and they will be a lot slower if they must reluctantly
depart from there. I must climb you like a tendril
of a climbing plant; see I can't stand without you
for it's always better to stay together for hard times.

Which Part of You Did I Leave Unloved?

So much time wasted wanting to be remembered
Ends with desire to be forgotten. — from 'The Wash' by Douglas Dunn

No use arguing for what I poured out of me into you,
like ink into an empty fountain pen

so that you could write grief if not happiness.
I wished you had taken the untrodden steps

– veiled in shrubberies – to tell me *I've discovered you,*
and I've started having a feeling for you but you

considered this a too-muchness for a worthless little loser.
I wanted you to know that my love was manifested

in every lie I told to squeeze your love into me.
But one thing is sure: you weren't gaslighted by me.

Maybe you were unsure that what anyone refers to
as a fact might always be proven true. Maybe I'd gotten

an error message from you. I wasn't ready for that.
I thought you'd change for the better, not for the worse,

that you'd understand my point made home on time.
I had the luxury of an idea: us forming an island;

now it's breaking apart and drifting. But I still enjoy
made-up concerns for you: *Please don't go braless*

in a skimpy tank top and joggers to deserted places
if I must add context to it. I'm not a body shamer.

Which part of you did I ever leave unloved?
I just don't like boll weevils to feed on cotton buds.

I still remember how fiercely I fought the urge
to be settling as a stone on a sea-bed for nothing.

Making Love in the Garo Hills

After the sleepless night, we first see the sun
gracefully down on green leaves of sal trees,
and the sunshower brings out their glitter
for the grand feast of Uncle Fox's marriage.

This morning is home to twittering day birds
and noisy squirrels busy with wild fruits.
As we walk deeper into hilly homesteads,
we come across a Garo woman washing

freshly pulled-out cassava roots in an oil
drum with its top cut halfway around it
and her man upturning an earthen cauldron
of roots with dry stuff on it for a fire boil.

A few yards upfront to the left, we meet
an old bearded, wrinkled man deeply brooding
in a bamboo chair by his growing tea plants.
But I have some other pressing thought.

In curiosity, I walk faster away in the drizzle
only to stand face to face with a treehouse
made of logs with no walls to fend off winds,
but it has a corrugated metal roof for rain.

The very moment I see it I imagine you lying
in there, naked with your alluring gesture
and with your lips moist with anticipation.
Everything's here to ignite the wild in us.

Times are undecodable but there's always
something about the way you look at me
even though I don't know what it is. Desire
or is it your weariness mistaken for it?

Every time you say we'd better drift apart
like continents, you gravitate toward me
as if toward a magnetic field. How can you
deny we fit together like pieces of a puzzle?

Twist around me like a twister in summer
though I can't enter the same you twice
and wash away the tiredness in every truth
in a stream or that hilly river's backwater.

How Can I Title This Poem on Love?

Hear me out on this, urgent as Munch's *Scream,*
or should you say, *To hell with it all?*
It's burning like E. coli in the urinary tract.

It's one thing to talk wisely about it,
quite another to feel it by yourself.
You can't shoot it straight off

with any double-barreled gun. It's
always like *Animali invisibili* but you may feel it
if you like to. I'm alone in memorizing

you in your absence. It's true –
I'd like to remember us in your presence.
In the rearview mirror, our love seems closer.

And did you see through the curtain
a bus entering the terminal when you sat
on the desk with your legs twining around me

or were you waiting for a knock on the door
when enjoying every bit of me
in the bathtub you might be thinking

– as if you had to right at that moment –
of your kids and hubby back at home?
The feelings of betrayal unraveled like balls of wool.

What was she? Not yet the sap rising in me.
A dud or an air defense system for the future?
She would know none of it, let alone

the intensity with which we said, *Let's do it*
with Cole Porter's swinging beat. I said
Once the door is closed, you are mine again.

My libido – a renewable energy – still lusts for you;
or does it need fracking like fossil fuels?
Interrupted by your getting frequent phone-calls,

I start losing you in your delight
over the prospect of orgasming with him at full tilt.
I wanted privacy for my pilgrimage in you:

you know the wetness made it holier for me
than the dryness in which you'd do
yours later on – titillating my anguish.

It was heaven on earth, imagining
you in a thick wood, us doing it standing up
or leaning on a bent plant under the sky –

our one witness. And twittering birds
could have been another. Were they
supposed to be the background music to match

with our sylvan play? No, everything was set
to be otherwise and I'm the reluctant actor in it.
How can I face the luminous dark

as you now prefer metal scrapings for my eyes?
Yet I feel love is neither a zero-sum game
nor touristy as townies' disinterred desires.

How can I title this poem on love?
Perhaps it's like a big ask or not so at all.
Should you call it sticky to seize winged seeds?

Am I a wildebeest crossing the river of crocs –
the river of memories with their jaws wide open?
Let me think: my past, my present, my future –

all pile up as slush on a publisher's desk.
Nothing chimes with my rhymes! As our love
sinks like a land bridge under the briny surge,

I wish you the much-awaited orgasmic cry.
The sooner you have it with him,
the quicker you can forget me behind the mist.

Like an Envelope Loves a Letter

After reading Cavafy's 'One Night'

I don't want to go back to the grumpy old days
that I passed without spooning you for warmth.
I don't remember who says the color of sadness is blue.
What use is so much of blue when I need more
of other colors? For I need green the color
of youthfulness that transforms graying trees in drought
or brown the color of your breasts perspiring in anticipation
of something enticing in the dead of a winter night
or the unnamed color of lovers' burning desire
for a river's ultimate libation into the sea. I'm tired,
weathering out your absence that tears through me
like a storm's downburst through a forest.
My body slowly unlearns your fingers' magic tricks.
So, the only time I think I would feel alive once again
is when we will make love on a creaking iron bed
on the squeaky wooden floor of a cheap hotel room
while people downstairs would feel uneasy.
What use is your nonperforming loan of promises
if you can't love me like an envelope loves a letter?

Who the Hell Benefits from Denials?

I

I know the depth of the injury I did to you;
you might need years to recover from it.
We might have expected a good coincidence

or a bit of what's known as luck, opposite
of what had happened. Having said that,
I know every single minute was a test,

and we failed. Pressure does funny things.
Yet I never fancied any chance against you
nor expected to luck out without you,

for a supersized ego shrinks in denials
like a balloon at a needle's slightest touch.
Who knows I won't be a dark horse this time,

not in anyone's radar, no favorite tag,
opposite of what's always been the case so far?
One upside to all this is that the harshest

words or unpredictability can't put me off
though I know desires bred in captivity
rarely survive in the wild as rock pigeons

take wing at the stink of a small Indian civet
prowling out on their corrugated tin roof.
Sometimes in this summer of suspicions,

I feel like being cool about everything else
as the white of water caltrops and chestnuts
growing profusely in freshwater wetlands.

But when you see tall towers falling in flames,
staying calm rather ignites the embers
you thought would always remain unignited.

II

By coincidence, we both loved wildlife.
Around your Granny's house in the rains,
we saw pond herons and purple swamphens

looking for flying barbs or any other fish
among lush aquatic plants in waterbodies.
And by coincidence again, we both relished

spotted snakeheads sautéed with turmeric
and smashed with dried chilies, onions,
and garlic. On a night as colorful as what

we call the Mediterranean moray – our code
name for raking the burning embers of lust –
you'd let me savor your breasts soft as ripe

jackfruit flakes and your marshy patch
further down below. The commotion on bed
would get so fierce the vase holding fresh

cut flowers quite often tumbled down
from the nightstand. Ah, the moment
I think about the nakedness of our bodies

and the nakedness of our entwined minds
everything seems to be soothing as a balm.
I think I'll never get done with all that.

Who the hell would kickstart the cleanup
for us? I say, *No one else.* So, is there a point
in breaking my heart smilingly? I am not

requesting you to accept me as a gem
you might have lost by mistake on the way,
rather as one humanly rife with imperfections.

Unfaithfulness a Two-way Street

I don't think I have my eyes on anything else
except the changes your body goes through.
At my touch, you fold inward like mimosa leaves.
It doesn't take longer to know I can't handle
pressure any better than when I learned: love is
inseparable from love-making. You don't know

I know who you are sleeping with. You've fallen
in love again, though not with me this time.
Yes, I too cheated on you when you wanted us
to be together like wet leaves. You didn't know
this gluey wetness wouldn't last. Now it's
your turn; this thought goes back a long way.

Far worse than being a cuckold like in old films,
I feel my life hands me just another drubbing
no less enticing than the first reassuring kiss.
Does it take too much to be of use to each other?
Be my new paramour, and let me be inside you
to know what it means to win every crisis with you.

As Insecure as Animals in the Anthropocene

It's cold outside, time to turn up the heat and get cozy indoors.
Who doesn't go great lengths to survive these cold winter nights?
Whatever we do together in this room will never get this Earth
out of its orbit nor force anyone to plummet into the sun.

In this teeth-chattering cold, I need you to wrap around me
in your body's warmth. It's always love o'clock for us in winter.
Just looking at your half-grown pomelos or fully ripe grapefruits
perks me up. I want to contemporize *Kamasutra* with the way

we exhaust ourselves, rubbing each other for a blissful shine.
If I were to tell you: the thing you can plant once and harvest
for years is love, would you believe it? What brings me
the heartsease is my love for you, and even a bushfire can't

spread faster than my fear of losing you. I don't want anyone's
opinion pieces right now for I don't want my dreams to break
down like sandcastles against breakers. The last thing I want
is any possibility of seeing your smirking face, visibly unkind!

I don't really know if I think about what you think about.
Before I have second thoughts, don't give me a hard time.
I can't afford to be angry. If so, I could say, You are beautiful
as a scary atlas moth! I couldn't say it much worse than this.

Maybe we are not on the same mission. Luckily you don't
have to listen to the cacophony of sand mining from the Bhogai
nor to think deeper into the damaging effects on the ecosystem.
Without you, I'm as insecure as animals in the Anthropocene.

Like the surprise of perfectly timed images, you'll be surprised
by the darkness of my heart about to reveal its acquired light.
Don't put your growing passion like coke back in the freezer.
Or if we need time, let's take a break before we are broken.

To thwart the unruliness in me, I need your autocracy
the only form of governance for me. Did I say this before?
I'd like to be happily handcuffed to you for the rest of my life
and make peace with the surprises that went wrong without you.

What Should I Tell My Wife on Our Tenth Wedding Anniversary?

I

In my childhood, as soon as I saw tengara
catfishes with eggs inside, displayed on
the lids of a bamboo-woven wicker basket

in the local fish market, I bought them.
I still remember my father brought home
a long whiskered catfish way taller than me

from a fishing village by the Jamuna. Stop,
why should I be ruining this special day
with such talk? Is it anyhow related to you?

I'm not a diversionist, stupid! The things
we knew would happen are happening
like the prophecy of sewage water running

after city's drains are unclogged in the rains.
I did the things I know I shouldn't have
done when you expected of your honey bee

to suck out nectar from your flower alone,
forgetting all about the nature of pollination
by bees roaming from flower to flower.

The germs of wickedness I might have
inherited from earlier adventures in the flesh:
they played filthy stuff over and over again

in my mind without my knowing of it,
and I cracked the hell of smutty jokes
about the foolishness of loyalty. And things

were utterly changed as if after the effects
of an overnight flood in the village by the river
but sediment remained as a bliss of fertility.

II

After the storm cleared, a new day dawned.
And we became transparent like glassware
though others couldn't see us. They still don't.

We have removed impurities from our gold.
And now I have what it takes to outgrow
my past, the fears that might have emerged

from their underground holts but the thicket
of my uncertainty about everything else
grows lush in spite of my pruning efforts.

I'm not lying through my teeth for I know
falsity waters no thirsting trees. Yet the harder
the grapevines have to struggle, the better

the wine. How can I deny the unalloyed
happiness that being in love with you
and your body has brought me? So I won't

body-shame you for your sagging breasts
nor for getting flabby around your waist
and having lots of stretch marks on your body.

Time and your love for kids did all that.
I won't go for a string of one-night stands.
For the last ten or so years with you, poetry

my other love is going flat out fantastic though
I don't care about the politics of numbers.
Call me any name you know me better by.

Without you, my life would have been
a sugarcane without sugar. Nowhere is more
homely than being here with you and kids.

Could I Make Love to You for the Last Time or Forever?

You are wearing a sari the color of guava leaves in the sun,
and your skin the color of a guava trunk with its bark
peeled off is the tightened skin of a festival drum.
Your fingers are peeled-off slender guava twigs.
I'm okay with these comparisons, for in my childhood
I used to spend time eating fruits from our guava tree
and look for its Y-shaped twig to make a slingshot
that you are like when you stand spreading out your legs.
Your breasts are plump guavas, let me have a big bite.

What I'm interested in is peeling you off like an onion
and sliding on your sweating flesh. The desire
that guides my life takes me back to you like a country
calls back the one who's exhausted living an expatriate's life.
Let me crush your lips' ripe fruit cluster of Indian spinach
and color the white of my life's accumulated frost.
I need the warmth of your skin against mine for survival.
I don't want to be ferried over anymore to a frigid woman
with who the dream of warmth is almost a disaster.

Words being inconsistent with desires, our bodies talked.
As they are no longer on speaking terms, I feel I'm
being swept away like iron filings without you nearby,
being pushed around by such fears while I want
to make love in the middle of dense jute plants at home
or on the moors' carpet of purple heather elsewhere.
I won't be lied to by your unlying body though I know
everything's not on the fun side of things anymore,
rather merciless as sunset's vermilion clouds in drought.

I'll tuck a water spinach flower into your untidy hair bun
after you wake up to my kisses at dawn. Waste
no time on how hungry I still remain, after you let me
eat the flesh of your red dragon fruit throughout the night.
I'm sorry I can't leave you to be happy with someone else:
your body is mine, your deep breathing is mine;
and just claim whatever I have because everything is yours.
I melt away in your rage; so let me live again in love.
Let me make love to you for the last time or forever.

Hiking in the Appalachians

Before triggering a firestorm
   over a governor's "hiking
the Appalachian Trail," I see people
   united against faithlessness —
but not on love. Love thrives on excuses;
   it dies under essentialist conditions.
I see love gleaming on glassy eyes
   of wolves; and ferocity from
our well-meaning eyes focuses less
   on love than on the profits we desire
by getting someone's love in trouble.
   The onslaught against it grinds on,
putting fears into the idea
   of having sad refuge in custody.
So, like a disappointed man
   strangled on every morality checkpoint,
he had to make an excuse, faking
   a trip in the lush wilderness
where I envision a moment of peace
   in a garter snake's jaws swallowing
a leopard frog for hunger; that frog
   must have taken in numberless
insects by its sticky tongue.
   His wife watched her hopes make
a crash-landing on a rugged terrain
   bordering a breakdown but
a convention can just as easily lose
   out to love that greens us as in
the transforming greenery. That peace
   in the backcountry vanishes,
anticipating sport-killings. Are we
   any better than sassy animals
protective of a waterhole, falling
   victim to this planet's rising water?

Note: Mark Sanford, Governor of South Carolina from 2003 to 2011, disappeared to 'hike the Appalachian Trail' in June 2009 but in reality he spent that time for his extramarital affair with an Argentine woman.

The Place Between Your Legs

the very thought of you
has my legs spread apart
like an easel with a canvas
begging for art
                    — rupi kaur

With seamy sex allegations you taunt
  me as I brace for an overhaul of
ways that didn't work for us.
  But when you say a few good
things about me — a slip of the tongue
  for sure, it seems like you took
down a book from an old termite-eaten
  wooden shelf and dusted it off
to read a few more brittle pages.
  This feels like heaven even though
I doubt myths about an afterlife.
  Your absence can ignite in me
an extremity like the rubbing of dry
  twigs the precursor to a wildfire
only you can put off. Blasted by
  the cold winds of winter, I see
how the misery of not having been
  inside you for a long time
punctuates all my sentences that I
  wrote in longhand on your body
throbbing with desire. If the place
  between your legs is a canvas,
let me breathlessly fill it with art.
  If it is an estuary, let me explore
its bottom. If it is a quicksand,
  let me go deeper and down into it
to find the thread-end of mysteries.

Obsessions

I

Honey, after school, I would throw my bag,
change my dress, and rush to visit
the workshop of an aged potter

to see how he made shapes out of clay
on his wheel. He talked to me
either while working or during breaks

and I sure knew he liked me.
His unfired pitchers lay upside down
to dry in the sun. Looking at them,

I could even imagine something else
or feel their cool softness on my fingers.
I mimicked him, playing with clay

on the corrugated tin roof
in the shade of our overhanging
custard apple tree or out in the sun.

II

Years later, a new obsession emerges:
I try to shape your clay-soft breasts
even though I know I'd fail.

I imagine drinking up the dew
from them on a clear winter morning.
If you play with the hose, you can

douse my body of fire in water. I love
the soapiness of your skin. Not having you
will be a pushover's bitter pill

to swallow or a ratsbane to a rat.
Then I'll feel like a winery out of action
by your lush vineyard. I'm no slyboots,

a dupable boor at best. I wonder
if my body will ever be undwellable,
if yours be an unenforced physical law?

PART THREE

EMBERS OF DISAPPEARANCE

Self-Portrait

Every sound I make is a crow's cawing.
Every word I use attacks all my loved ones like a porcupine.
Every step I take is either a misreading or a backtracking.
But every remorse I just want to heave away
sticks to me like my skin, with no bother about any deadline.
The air I breathe in, as if wishing for an increase on my payday,
is the fume of toxic chemicals.
Epitomes of what I look for are long captured in cells.

Every truth is an insult to every sugary lie;
it risks the gang rape by a crowd of lies on the running bus
as if it had invoked acerbic curses from the sky.
The punishment for my temper tantrum
is not uncalled for, nor by any means superfluous.
It justifies the prudent pull at my scrotum.
What should be my modus operandi on the raceway
when all must try techniques are scenes in a dull screenplay?

Every pleasure I manage turns into bitterness.
I get only what I've never wanted,
things scarier than corpses covered in diplomatic finesse.
Drought turns up as I join the masses praying for rain.
Coldness slinks in when I need someone undaunted
to give me the warmth of her arms, to dull my pain.
I'm not Oedipus misfortune loved so much
but surely the one far from a small rabbit hutch.

Requiem for the Undead

in memory of those displaced in wars

Stalks of wheat and barley with their hairy roots
are drying before they get crowned in gold.
Their husks the rough skin of old-wrinkled hags.
Bullet shells no manna for one's hunger-filled bowel.

Warlords are avaricious; they care only for honey.
Houses the beehives on fire; eggs, larvae – all gone.
People the fleeing bees get their wings burned.
Dreams die with the loss of wings. Will they fly again?

A mossed pond stinks with its belly-up dead fish.
Did poison ask to be poured in the dead of night?
A desert greens with corpses planted as seedlings.
Did dry sands wish to be washed out with blood?

This time not for olives and almonds; what for?
Towers of Silence, and the excarnating beasts.
Griffons gyrating overhead, only to swoop down
on the unburied dead scattered on cornfields.

Nothing drops, only eggs of ruin hatched up in labs –
more alive than a scenic waterway through hills.
God hoots with cheers for the only genuine play.
Sophocles flares with envy and slips away in shame.

Weary footfalls, the oars knifing the watery flesh.
The dreams that linger are burst-out bubbles
or hollowed-out conches washed on alien shores.
Batons, barbed wares, and the cold greet the future.

The clatter of almost empty plates at refugee camps –
a bulletin on how to weed out the roots of ruin.
It makes desires rhyme with the fluttering green.
It stops the desert eating up the veldt. Ah, the music!

Blood Blossoms

in memory of poets dead in wars

Carry my crying spirit till it's weaned
To do without what blood remained these wounds. — Wilfred Owen

I

In every century, I see a creeper with blood-blossoms —
looking better than aurora borealis. It lives on wars.

Am I the only one who sees black-tarped trucks come
stealthily as inamoratos in the silence of night
and strappingly like tanks in broad daylight?

II

This creeper is no picky eater, it eats all up. Locals
across the world cry all are becoming souls too soon.

What do I know of the souls as undulating
as crops on a mountainous terraced slope
or as vigorous as trained fishing cormorants?

III

This creeper doesn't bother about a global apology.
It doesn't know any backing off on its onslaught.

Not all are skygazers, but all are earthgazers
getting its blossoms merged into every canvas.
Our dreams are falling apart and totally on edge.

IV

Everything's baffling as the behavior of a wildfire.
What happens next is hard to predict. Bees,

fed by the creeper's honey, will hunt you down
– wherever you hide, however long it takes –
and lay a bouquet of gratitude on each hasty dead.

V

Griffons circle overhead, waiting upon us:
the stink of a cancerous carrion in each of us.

We foolishly thought of it as valued as love
saved up snug in our hearts' safety lockers.
How can we hide it now from their scavenging eye?

VI

Memory is enough salt on Ovid's wounds —
Tristia as eerie as ignes fatui on swamps at night.

And just for a coronet of blood-blossoms
the nefarious killjoys let loose termites in a woodlot,
poop out in ennui. Nukes need not even be fired.

VII

And at times, pumice instead of words comes
out of my mouth as if it were the volcanic crater.

Should my life imitate art? Or my art
the humanity halfway down the road to hell?
This perplexity is no less prized than asteroids.

To Keith Douglas

I

I cannot simplify you. Your words, though simple,
crush me with their enormous weight
of beauty and dread woven by the same thread.
The extinction not of the self but of the soul,

its very thought ruffles my mind today.
The hard-won ease defies its moorings. This century
is no less the forest of graves strewn beneath our feet
and I sense the anguish of muffled laments

as our only giving to music. The old jaws are still open.
Greed and distrust are our two open eyes,
blinking at every gain they can. For poets
these are still the subjects that fuel our hearts –

our raisons d'être, though drifting like driftwood
on surging waves of our expanding decay.

II

At times it seems opinions welcome us to graves
through the gallows, and we greet them back.
I wonder if your death was needless and if you
reburied at Tilly-sur-Seulles need to escape forever

like words from the confinement of white pages,
to fall as the rain predicting the futility of things
we do in good faith. Yes, an ease would have
easily been won if outright lies had been told for cover

but we tongue-tied nerds locked in a tragedy of fate
– knowing rupestrine weeds still flower in summer –
choose the easiest way to be ridiculed by gun-barrels,
canonized as the undamned by an uncertain shore.

No, I cannot simplify anything, not even this life
that prays for swines' health and calms us in elegies.

The War Poets

I flip through the pages of their poems –
a mosaic of bullets to walk on. I feel
uneasy about their sad acceptance of horrors –
the very air they had to breathe in & out.

They feel like abandoned military posts
at forest edges under the full moon
or at best like sunlight streaking through
a castle window with the roof blown off.

I listen to an incorrigible music of screams,
life-inducing and indomitable even
in the face of outright annihilation.
Even if they thought the unforgiving frost

wouldn't thaw, they braved an unflinching
tryout with their blood gushing forth.
They saw all bridges going down except
the one that still arches over human hearts,

hitting back at all the disconnecting wars.
Whatsoever, their belief in art didn't
let the world tighten around their necks.
Like blotting paper, I soak up their courage.

Boris Pasternak

A cloud-dweller I am, unharmed, according to
the tyrant with a fat cockroach for his mustache.
But my boots get soiled in the slushy mud,
and harm is rightly spelt in my anxiety.

Everyday I see the sun up with new threats
and down with its success stories of intimidation.
Every night the moon does a nurse's duty
with its silver-tinged ointment to rub on wounds,

but they are obstinate, refusing to be cured.
I think this cycle will continue before I'm
reported dead. If I get to the very bottom of it,
I'm sad because sadness cannot be news anymore.

I must say I'm not unlike an unhinged window
of a vacant house with cold air-currents coming in.
I'm wintered-out, dreaming to be summering
like 20-somethings with unbridled emotions.

Keeping all of what I have inside in check freezes
the warmth of keeping them. At Peredelkino,
I look at furrows in the snow as if Pushkin's
sprightly lines denying the cold, yet the more

I look out the more I think of a shivering rat
that sneaked into my cabin for shelter, running
from the wild wind spying over Siberia. I feel
good about that little grace. I listen to the wind's

notes as poems whose fire I loved to rekindle
against the frost of everything now threatens
to grill me as if with a skewer. But I won't be
surprised if the world might say I was unharmed.

To a Gunman

in memory of Dhaka terror attack

Like the mysterious rise of your enemy's language,
I'm simply out there where love gets voted down,
where hate crimes are only other things on the rise,
where misfits like me either remain misfits all their life
or make headlines only as upturned cockroaches.
If I ever trembled before your gun-barrel, I'd say:
Before you are done with me, stay with me a bit longer.
Do me a favor – wait a little with me to watch squirrels

climb up a tree over there by the lake. Look, how smart
and death-defying they are, hoarding nuts into that
tree's gnarled twigs hollowed by termites and swept
clean by the south wind. The music of ripples on the lake
soothes their minds like rain. By the way, did you know
rain is the buzzing of bees vertically landing on flowers?
The moment I think of flowers I see the redness of roses
immaculate as the blood you will spill today. It's as

if you'd by mistake pour coffee onto my writing.
Once I reined in the leash of my unrest by looking
at those smart squirrels bringing nuts to their babies.
I often come here to detox my evils. Shower me,
if you like, with bullets as if to water dying roses of my blood –
ink for your death script. Take this blood as my offering.
Even though no holy verse is ever written in blood,
only love gets bloodstains out as sunlight does darkness.

Prayers to the God of Jihadists

I

Are you sure you of the Jihadists
aren't the same old One for us commoners?
We never denied our God's gifts.
But we simply refuse yours –
they are bombs wrapped in florid cellophanes.
Mistakenly, my son took one
and got strewn as gravel on streets instead.
I buried one bag of his burst remains
with tears from our ordinary eyes,
with prayers to the One who gave us life.
Oh, one of your gifts killed my only son –
my one seed wasted in the drought of this desert.
Are you sure you are the same as our One?

II

Keep us the destitute in your prayers.
Oops, I'm sorry you don't have to pray, do you?
Or do you need to pray to the Jihadists
so that they can strike obedience
in every heart like a fiery spark
so that you can prosper in your servants' fear –
a fungus sucking life from the rot?
They say you are the All Powerful
but you need them to protect yourself
from a single infidel's slur on your character.
I'll pray to our God so that you can feel safe.
Because your feeling unsafe doesn't ensure safety to us.
Build your abode with quality bricks and iron.

III

Are you short of your messengers of death?
Are these Jihadists your new recruits,
your new conscripts in time of this prolonging war?
They plant seeds into our daughters by force;
they waste our daughters like weeds
even before our daughters flower.
At times, our daughters are sold in the flower market.
We all feel good our daughters are slowly learning
how to milk each Jihadist's swollen teat.
I pray you recruit some messengers of life.
On these ruins amid a flesh-rotting stench,
we all love life to flower –
the only perfume to nullify all stench.

IV

Our God prefers tolerance to fruits of war.
Cowardice is a vice when bravery means
slitting throats by a sharp knife
on thirsty sands. Maybe you love to see
the body without the head wriggling on blood,
the worthy charm like the mystery of Jesus –
a son conceived without a father's seed,
like the mystery of Moses passing
through a sea thrust open like a watery door
as if a Jihadist's water-divining tongue
parting my daughter's dry cunt lips
for the grand arrival of His Holy Dickhead.
I pray, "Help me understand the mystery of all mysteries."

V

Did you, too, create time like our God did
in six days, only to rest on the seventh?
Time, our sole sympathizer beside God,
– often out of its inspired whimsy – scribbles
on water and even engraves on granites
all of its griefs given as gifts.
The mountains we see over there
are manifestations of its griefs thrust up
instead of molten lava
and the oceans we bathe in are its tears
gathered in a mass. Yet, O God of the Jihadists,
we all pray let us dream of a skyfall
of bliss instead of burst splinters.

VI

We are boulders iced on a rugged mountain,
unaffected for ages unless moved
by blessings like winds or quakes.
I can't stand the stonification of my griefs.
Get me the bliss of breaking into pieces,
dividing the burden. Are you sure
you aren't the old One for us commoners?
I've already forgotten the smell of my children's blood.
Even then our friends with a different God in their hearts
always suspect us. Spare me the pain.
This is my petition. I'm planning to make
another to the God of the Crusaders as well.
I don't know how many Gods I need to pray to.

VII

And the Crusaders vowed revenge on your Jihadists.
Before they get "wasted in the outhouse,"
we don't want to be mistaken for them.
Tell your Jihadists not to lecture us on wreckage,
not to slit the throats of those who write;
writing gets their fingers fit for prayers if you like.
Our God of Peaceful Fragility must have
contrived a simpler scheme of things for us;
don't rebuke our God who cries out like us in despair,
and even gladly accepts defeat to a little rat,
only to make it feel victorious among the ratters.
Are you sure you aren't the same old God?
Am I praying to our dear old God?

Worries at a Hilltop Resort

I'm lying on a beach-style outdoor bench at a hilltop resort,
enjoying the fresh air from all around and the warm
sunshine at this time of winter even though I know
bombs are falling like hail on some parts of the world
and deaths are being recorded in destiny's logbook.
I'm holding my four-month-old daughter drooling
and crawling on me while somewhere the legs of toddlers
are already broken before they learn to toddle.
My four-and-a-half year-old son is scampering here

and there to catch dragonflies resting on the blades
of long unmown grass by the lake while his yearmates
gather empty artillery shells for sale in local scrap markets
because buying bare necessities are part of their struggle
to keep heads above ruins. My wife is in the shower
to wash off her drowsiness and the tiredness of travel
while desperate mothers seek refuge for their kids –
their only hopes. My dreams of having a rest are gone,
and here stalk my nightmares that are not wizen-faced

witches in a bamboo-grove but diplomatic acrobatics,
political dogfights and smear-campaigns: all these make
humanity live on life support before it gets flatlined.
Schizophrenics set loose across the globe say:
bombs every now and then are necessities like food,
the scarcity of which spells chaos, is it a disguiser's cynosure?
What will I do with a catcaller's life of smut and booze
or a parroter's unuttered embargo on questions?
How can I write poems and think of beauty alone?

Let the Ashes Speak

You, yes, you who train your eyes to be shockproof
see so many unburied dead rotting everywhere.
And those who flee their houses flaming up in fire
to get across bullet-strewn lands, mine-punctuated waters
say, *Don't look here. Art's fine refinements are elsewhere.*

You always get your ears to listen to those who never
set to music children's cries on hungry nights
and the rain falling on camps' tattered plastic.
If curious by chance, you ask the refugees, they
say, *Don't ask for answers anymore. Let the ashes speak.*

Persecution

for Robert Pinsky

INSTEAD OF AN EMAIL

I

I carefully flip through the pages of your books.
You look lastingly calm on the surface but I see the bits
wearing away from beneath your stony bulk.

You take sustenance from the roots of your Jewishness,
which isn't simply for the cover of *The Figured Wheel*.
Who unlearns the Holocaust horrors? Memory

is Ovid's wounds in Tomis, a wildfire eating trees
and shitting ashes and tall charcoals. And here I am,
a long-barreled gun loaded with mistakes. Something

gets pressed under a double drum road roller.
I strive against the tyranny of thoughts. (I need
facelifting, as crucial as packets of silica gel in a shoebox.)

Yet every thought seems to be a wind-coarsened twig
on which my feelings grow as leaves. What am I?
A campaign for the Albigensians' love outside marriage?

Or the home-grown contempt for it? I'm not durable
as acid-free archival-grade paper. I'm recycled, made
through pulping and de-inking, rough fibers poking through.

II

I'm at best a foothill at the base of a mountain range,
with no hope at all to be one of its highest peaks.
Even my grandparents didn't start seeing each other

when you crawled out of your crib toward your parents'
bed, and my father was not even a dream for them.
When your name was pinned to the sky, I wasn't

even an embryo in my mother's womb. Yet the distance
– whether of a place or a time or anything else –
somewhat gets bridged as some incorrigibles say.

III

You sent your books without any inscriptions
like oiled peacock feathers we kids lovingly put inside.
Is it because of the distance we were born with?

Yes, you're now a senior white American Jew
and I'm a junior brown Bangladeshi "secular"
(even "secular" means in the West a cover for "terrorist").

I read out "Crossing Brooklyn Ferry" to my students
and like Whitman don't give a damn about distance.
Can't we ever say like him, *Distance avails not?*

But the distance waits in ambush like an assassin
and plans like an abortionist to kill the embryo
of our liberating trust, shaking the very base

of my telescopic love for you and for your poems
sparklingly pinned to my night sky. I'm earthier,
so my love will be soiled with suspicions.

In the wake of the Confederate flags flying
o'er the land of the free and the home of the brave!
I know brown won't ever be de-browned to white.

I'm a genealogist, cracking the encryption codes
of all those suspicions under my critical lenses.
Oh, don't let color and culture make distance between us.

Elsewhere lines of sanity are now increasingly blurred.
Erich said *Hear, O Israel!* A new Holocaust is raging on.
So between an anvil and a hammer I stammer:

For Jews in Hitler's war my sad tears drip,
Also for kids bombed out in the Gaza Strip.
Not anti-Semitic but you know Zionists never get it.

You're no longer a fiddler on the roof. Our hearts
are urns of Auschwitz's ashes. Let our conscience
scramble to intercept our criminal silences for survival.

AFTER AUSCHWITZ

When you say "seniority, color, nationality and religious politics —
all of which we can't avoid even if we try to" I agree.
Those "grand narratives" or assigned windows. Yet we can look out them.
                                    — from Pinsky's email

I

The Exodus, the Assyrian exile and then Babylon.
The Pharaoh's order: Hebraic newborns to die
in the Nile. With the Third Reich came the worst.

Now with the last Reich in ruins, at Auschwitz
— the Nazis called it the "Final Solution" to Jews —
strewn with memories of transport trains

crammed with captives for "concentration"
— a euphemism for slaughter, of corpses,
bones and human ashes from its crematorium,

of bone crushing machines for the striped clothes,
and of Zyklon B in the Gas Chambers,
liberated by the Red Army in that cold January,

we need a new art of cartography, to map intolerance
from the Alexandrian pogrom to the Holocaust,
and at last a declaration of beauty in life.

II

After Auschwitz, we read Anne's diary
and the wealth of dark texts on innocent pages,
saw Olère's paintings like "Arrival of a Convoy,"

listened to Shostakovich's Op. 113 "Babi Yar"
or Górecki's Op. 36 "Symphony of Sorrowful Songs"
and I still see the specters of paranoid disorder.

History changes its course like a wild river
and tells that we almost never learn from it:
new killing fields unroll their cold carpets of ruin.

III

I'm sick of all these pogroms. We've had enough.
You know these didn't happen to Jews alone.
Black July, anti-Sikh riots, Babri Mosque, Gujarat,

anti-Hindu riots, Ramu in this sediment-rich delta,
anti-Rohingya unrest across the Naf...my heart bleeds.
What does despair get wrong about? Yes, there are

"assigned windows," waiting to be thrust open
to let the radiance light up the darkness inside us;
often late but still not too late to be good.

When you say "Yet we can look out them," I bring myself
up from despair's black-hole, against all likelihoods.
Anxiety then gets paved with new anticipations.

O Clio, history has nothing to do with sleep;
in daylight we see its spoils as that fleece in Colchis,
at times in cellophane wraps. Yet, every time

we clear shells and skeletons to let flowers bloom
– a reminder of what the flowerbuds went through –
there's the feeling survivors had, when rescued at long last.

Yes, poets go on as the lowest paid, if not otherwise.
Some of us elsewhere in life's deadliest camps
still die of exhaustion or starvation – a reward indeed

for tilling the white space of pages, in hopes of
manna during the travels in our own deserts. Or
for a posthumous glory like light at the dark tunnel's end?

Some remain tyrants' sycophants in their affluence.
Most others don't just write about the flame of history,
we live it. Some of us die burned like Jews. Yet, we team up,

as if nothing happened at all, to say life is beautiful
– even though the season of ruin sets in around us –
to make gray a mother of all surrealist colors.

A Signature of Piss

You're beautiful because for you, politeness is instinctive, not a marketing campaign.
I'm ugly because desperation is impossible to hide.

– Simon Armitage

I

With a squirrel's unrest, I wanted to be calm,
like a forest where winds rarely storm into its leaves,
like a lake where fish rarely leap and dive back into its water.

But night brought me an earthquake to take me
deeper into its bowels. Day wanted to leave me
crunchy like charcoal. Everything's a twister to twist me

chokingly. Calmness is a country I've never visited.
Eyes in their first extremity or their last never fancy
things unsafe as cornice fall on the leeward sides,

ears never the immaculate music of crash. Yet
my eyes and ears are forcibly glued to nightmares,
the ones rival armies did in the old or new Crusades.

After crippling losses, insanity reigns. It makes
my non-partisan self even lonelier, awaiting
persecution. Should I be cozying up to nightmares?

II

Yes, the rhetoric of protest often heats up like politics
with no integrity at the core. Then I feel like breeding
American Pit Bull Terriers to fuck the bastards

who write on raped little angels, bombarded cities,
creepy excuses for WMDs, or whatever feels fit
to show in great words that they care. Squeeze

them hard. But no love will spill over to quench
your drought. They go from defiant to yielding
to the profitable bait. I slip out of their protesting line.

III

In Berkeley you said you'd left a signature of piss –
at best a little fun out in the open. An amusement,
from your serious self. You've learned to use

the language of decorum even for smutty yellers
in their newly-energized brawls: *Burn the thing down,
fuck the hell out of it and then see what happens.*

I appreciate your decent protest. Simple as that.
But the charm of complexity consumes me.
And I start wondering how one can always

utter grievances in such exquisite gentleness,
the words of dissent in the grammar of approval.
Though I plunge to a decade low when confusions breed,

I shout to my surprise: *Listen, I'm a little cockroach;*
and all I say is – I badly need a new approach. A shocker?
I can see darkness brewing up breezily in light

and even happily lose its memory like a goldfish.
Those thick-headed brutes forget that daylight
silvers the dark corners of dissent in my mind.

Yes, I'm still a verb in the grammar of dissent,
a shuttle on the loom, from active to passive
and vice versa to make a dress with dissenting threads:

my work is its memory against forgetting. I wonder:
Am I the dullest, the sleepiest non-arguing cock?
Do I deserve an award for "Best Laughing Stock?"

Comedians brazen out the shit of their screenplays;
only the brutes with their sticky sugarcoated lies cheer
the hell out of us. But I'd rather love to stay clean.

I'm done with the baring of their canine teeth at me.
Whatever it takes, I won't slink into my tortoise shell.
I'd leave a signature of piss on every deal they make.

The Return

for Ngũgĩ wa Thiong'o

I

Perhaps I'll come back like a salmon fish
to that same estuary again;
I may wish to see my newcomers swim on that old stream.

Or perhaps I'll stay away like a statue hewn out of a huge rock,
far away from my grandparents' mountain,
on another longitude, alone under another sky.

But the return doesn't mean the return of my body,
something more, beyond five senses for sure.
Who knows if distance is just steam in a lid-locked pressure cooker?

II

As my body gets dry like a split bamboo this summer
the sound coming off it like cacophony on the air
I remember the old gossipy days. My mind was soft

like a bamboo shoot – is that only the past? Or is it
the ripe bamboo's fond love for its memories still green?
I still remember that over my roots under my leaves,

a toad took shelter during the rains. A few days later,
a snake came to announce its rights and satisfied its hunger.
Necessity flicked its forked tongue and ate me, too.

III

The taste of crescent-shaped rice-dumplings on a winter morning,
the broth of a curry with swamp barbs and leaf amaranth,
a little spicy rice flour slightly fried with margosa leaves on a
  moonless night –

I'm wondering if all these memories have turned pale
under the stone of distance? Perhaps so.
Or perhaps I've lost all those memories, like marbles

lost in knee-deep mud from the knot of my lungi
while bathing in a large pond. But some fossils
of that time are still preserved in my mind's museum.

IV

Bathing in a canal, she got a tiny shrimp
entangled in her hair bound tight by a red ribbon.
From then on, I used to call her *The Shrimp Girl*.

Sitting on a land aisle between cornfields, she sang,
letting her goats graze on. I clasped her breasts
from behind her and said: *These wood apples are soft.*

She held her head low in shame. Who knows where she is now?
Her mind was soft like a sapodilla, and I've remained
the fruit-eating bat all my life, here and abroad.

V

Then I flapped my wings and flew to another language –
the country you can't catch hold of in a net
of longitudes and latitudes. Then I forgot

the biological pull of the language I'd learned in my mother's womb.
Some say I've lost the silver of Gangetic ailias,
as I swam in the other water, caught in weeds.

Of course, I talk about the other way around. Trust me:
One can't be a different man with a different dress on.
You've just stopped before it, sadly never beyond it.

A Food Enthusiast Reflects on the Clash of Civilizations

I'm not the one who lectures on clashes.
  My mouth simply waters

at items of my culinary preference:
  a plate of steamy rice

with crunchy fried pumpkin flowers
  with a pinch of salt sprinkled on them,

then Ganges river sprats cooked
  in mustard oil with ribbed gourd slices

and peeled jackfruit seeds,
  then prawns cooked with taro stolons

and a bit of tamarind added to it
  for fear of having a throat itching;

and in between the items, I'll love
  a refrigerated drink of yogurt

blended with spices and mint leaves.
  These I'd definitely prefer for my last supper

if I'm charged with conspiracy
  and the verdict is capital punishment.

The Photographer

I've been remanded, denied bail and put
  behind bars like a convict. I still
remember how they stormed my house

  when dawn in its infancy was just peeping,
and how blood from my punched-out nose
  drenched my dress. The pain is –

pared down to the minimum, I'm limping
  in this cell without my camera. Every day
left at my doorstep a pile of photographs

  the way a young mother leaves her illicit
newborn in a refuse dumpsite. They thought
  snaps were illicit without their consent

while I didn't, for I shed light equally
  on all of them as proof of truths,
each of which is a cure for our muteness;

  and falsity never hesitates to do anything
to make it even worse. I want caged birds
  to sing their dreams out loud so that captors

feel the horror of wings being of no use.
  Palmyra palm trees, though rooted,
make wings of their fronds. And only freedom

  gets us on the wing. But in this country,
rules from their laboratory rain down on us
  clay subjects and wash away what we made

solid with labor. I wonder if they'll wise up
  to the light brewing under darkness.
Those mute photographs will be vocal soon.

In the Election Year

I

Words rub against themselves to get the gloss
and be pulpy like curvy beauties —
to be chosen in political parties' manifestos,
to be adored by swing voters who wait for changes.
Words are tricky agenda in disguise,
willing to ride the tips of voters' tongues.
But if they fail the test on the election day,
they might be laughed away for another term.

II

The sale of firearms on the black market,
the scale of pamphlets and posters,
and the rate of secret killings rise up
despite mikes blaring out enticing promises.
Banknotes fly with campaign slogans,
and needy folks sell their votes several times.
We are *classical*, for we take things as they are:
say, elections are there only to be rigged.

III

With shut mouths, we expect the change-up
to come over to us like a good dictator;
that's the height of our wishing
for good tidings. The world is looking for
crevices to sneak into but they are
heavily plastered. Our suffocation is a genie
hidden away in a lamp, and there's no Aladdin
among us, not even the faintest hope.

Education

Your efforts must never produce learned monsters, skilled psychopaths or educated Eichmanns. – Haim G. Ginott (1922–1973), a Holocaust survivor

If it trains you for monetary purposes alone,
  driving your gaze into the narrow lanes of worldly benefits,
if it doesn't go beyond the limits of individual horizons
  to explore the things that have so far remained mysterious
  and unresolved, not to exploit people's weaknesses,
if it only sharpens your educated cleverness
  to exercise brutality on someone else's neck,
if you don't think the lack of love anywhere is a threat to love everywhere,

if your political pride no one ever doubts is to never apologize
  for the bullets and cannonballs sown across the world,
if in times like this social distancing at its worst,
  you don't hesitate to tear down all the morals and values
  your ancestors might have taken centuries to painstakingly build up,
if you never act as quickly when the world around you
  breaks apart in chaos as you did when your love of
being gossiped about in the magazines and media was questioned,

if you never think the flip side of what you learned in school
  is that you free up no time for others, only yourself,
if you always want to keep your poetry quite creatively
  opaque like a frosted glass door even when
  your black neighbors are routinely mutilated by hate,
if you heat up your ignorance and decide you sure as hell won't do
  anything about the coloreds drowning in the white sea,
if you stand like an Indian mast tree, seeing them all fall on prickly poppies,

if you never wake up soaked in night sweat,
  worrying about the rise of salinity in fishing canals and rivers,
if your coal power plant never lets you care about
  sundaris, river and milky mangroves, screw pines,
  cannonball nuts, and nipa palms hiding swamp tigers in the Sundarbans,
if your dog-eared pages and the scholarly air of your gray hair
  do not aid the rallying cry for letting nature take care of itself,
know for yourself that your learning is a downhill slide to destruction.

Photo credit: Ohidujjaman Beeplaub

SOFIUL AZAM has three published poetry collections: *Impasse* (2003), *In Love with a Gorgon* (2010), *Safe under Water* (2014), and has edited *Short Stories of Selim Morshed* (2009). His work has appeared in *Prairie Schooner, Pirene's Fountain, North Dakota Quarterly, The Ibis Head Review, The Ghazal Page, Cholla Needles, Poetry Salzburg Review, Orbis, The Cannon's Mouth, Postcolonial Text*, and elsewhere. Some poems are anthologized in *Two Thirds North, fourW: New Writing 28, Journeys, Caught in the Net*, among others. He is working on two poetry collections *This Time, Every Time* and *Days in the Forested Hills*. He currently teaches English at World University of Bangladesh, having taught it before at other universities.

www.**salmon**poetry.com